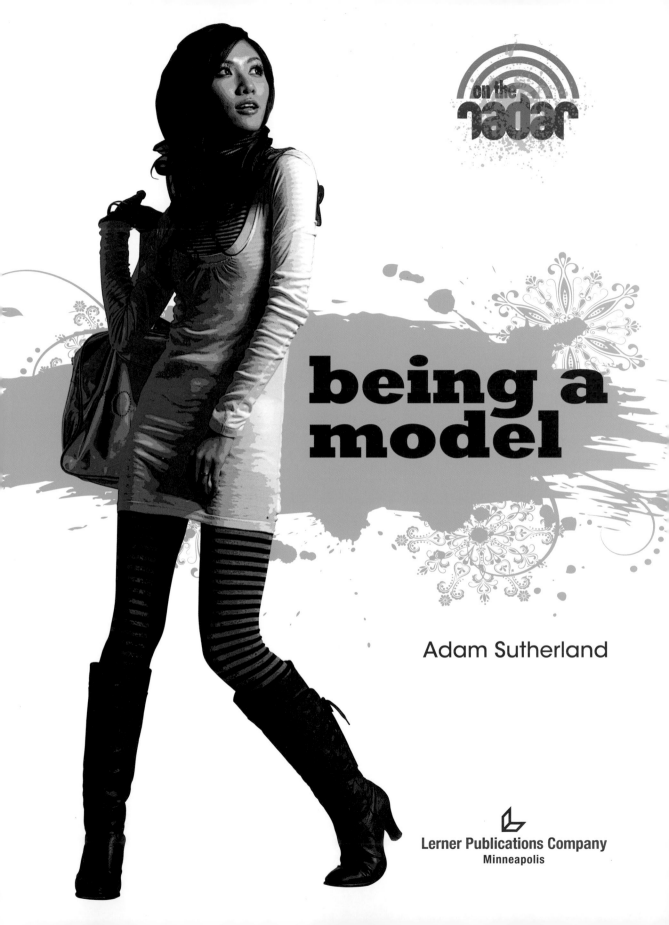

on the
radar

being a
model

Adam Sutherland

Lerner Publications Company
Minneapolis

First American edition published in 2013 by Lerner Publishing Group, Inc. Published by arrangement with Wayland, a division of Hachette Children's Books

Lerner Publications Company
A division of Lerner Publishing Group, Inc.
241 First Avenue North
Minneapolis, MN U.S.A.

Website address: www.lernerbooks.com

Library of Congress Cataloging-in-Publication Data

Sutherland, Adam.
   Being a model / by Adam Sutherland.
     p.   cm. — (On the radar : awesome jobs)
   Includes index.
   ISBN: 978-0-7613-7782-5 (lib. bdg. : alk. paper)
1. Models (Persons)—Vocational guidance—
Juvenile literature. I. Title.
HD6073.M77S88 2013
746.9'2023—dc23   2011052665

Manufactured in the United States of America
– CG – 7/15/12

Acknowledgments: AP: Damian Dovarganes 16; Joy Fatoyinbo: 26–27, 26br, 27bc, 27br, back cover; Getty: Chris Moore/Catwalking 30br; Gemma Howorth: 2t, 25; Istock: Joel Carillet 11r; Rex USA: David Fisher 17; Shutterstock: Subbotina Anna 14–15, Apollofoto 1, 10r, Jorge Cubells Biela 4–5, Cinemafestival 21b, Conrado 11tl, Olga Ekaterincheva 31, Helga Esteb 2b, 18, Ben Heys 6–7, Geoffrey Jones 3br, Lev Radin 11bl, Julian Ribinik 12–13, Stocklight 20–21, Mayer George Vladimirovich 30tr, 31, Debby Wong 2c, 22–23, Natalia Yeromina cover, 8, 9r, Serg Zastavkin 28–29.

Main body text set in
Helvetica Neue LT Std 13/15.5.
Typeface provided by Adobe Systems.

cover stories

24 REAL-LIFE STORY
Discover how your hands, lips, or feet could be your fortune!

22 POSTER PAGE
Take a look at one of the world's leading male models.

30 BIG DEBATE
Should size 0 be banned from catwalks?

18 STAR STORY
Get the latest on model and actress Scarlett Johansson.

thepeople

16	**READ ALL ABOUT IT** Hollywood models
18	**STAR STORY** Scarlett Johansson
20	**TOP FIVE** Most successful models
22	**POSTER PAGE** Tyson Beckford
24	**REAL-LIFE STORY** Star hands
26	**FIVE-MINUTE INTERVIEW** Joy Fatoyinbo

themoves

| 10 | **ZONE IN** Working the look |
| 12 | **PICTURE THIS!** Front row |

thetalk

4	**FEEL IT** Showtime!
6	**ALL ABOUT** Strike a pose!
8	**THE LINGO** Model speak
14	**RECORD BREAKERS** Action figures
28	**PULL A NUMBER** Vital statistics
30	**BIG DEBATE** Size 0 on the catwalk: yes or no?
32	**FAN CLUB** Get more info
32	**INDEX**

SHOWTIME!

You're out of bed before dawn and at the site of the show early, ready for the hours of preparation before the catwalk starts. You are nervous but excited. You feel butterflies in your stomach. You're ready to impress. This is a big show for one of the top designers in the fashion industry—someone you've always wanted to model for. You're determined to make a really good impression, and you hope to be back on the catwalk for him next season too.

Get the look

You take your place in front of the mirror alongside a dozen other girls. Two hours of hair and makeup lie ahead. People are buzzing around you like autograph hunters around a pop star. While someone does your eyes, an assistant is working on your lips and two more are working on your hair. Next come the outfits. You'll be modeling quite a few, and quick changes are essential. The dressers are like a Nascar pit crew: everyone has his or her own job to do, working like a well-oiled machine. Even the most elaborate outfits are on and off in a matter of seconds.

Walk the walk

Here goes! You're in the first outfit—a floor-length skirt and towering heels—and it's time to hit the catwalk. No matter how many times you do this, you can't get used to it. It's a huge buzz. The adrenaline makes you light-headed. Your mouth is dry, and your heart's trying to beat its way out of your chest. You take a deep breath and step onto the runway. In an instant, your training and experience take over. You move almost unconsciously through your routine—to the end of the catwalk, turn, pause, and back.

Back for more

The show has gone extremely well. The audience has been applauding throughout. At the close, it's like the end of a rock concert. The crowd is on its feet, cheering and calling for the designer. He grabs your hand, walks out onto the catwalk, and takes a bow. You're so proud, you're walking on air. It's a fantastic feeling—one you'll never forget.

Go and see

When models are not in front of a camera, they are often expected to attend castings or visit potential new clients or photographers. These visits are called "go-sees." They are the least glamorous part of the job. Models can spend an hour or more waiting for a two-minute meeting.

STRIKE A POSE!

For many young people, modeling looks like an incredible job. Wearing great clothes, traveling the world . . . and getting paid for it! But like most jobs, it involves a lot of hard work and dedication to reach the top. Modeling is made up of different people playing key roles. Here are some of them.

On the books

Models are represented by model agencies. The agency is responsible for finding work for a model, negotiating the model's fees, and introducing the model to new brands, photographers, and magazines. The agency manages the model's career. A fashion model works with only one agency and does high-end runway work and ads. Commercial models can be on two or three agencies' books. They do work for consumer products, clothing, and catalogs.

Booked up

A model's schedule is organized by a model booker. Depending on the size of the agency, one or a dozen bookers could be working together. Each booker looks after a certain number of models and builds up a strong working relationship with them. Fashion models contact their booker at the end of every working day to find out their schedule for the following day. Commercial models are contacted by their agency if they are required to attend a casting for a particular job.

Finding faces

Scouting is very important. Fashion agencies send scouts to large events, such as music festivals, to search for new faces. Scouts are looking for the "next big thing," the new Tyra Banks or Kate Moss. They are often searching for something out of the ordinary, but they always want height. Women must be 5 feet 8½ inches (1.7 meters) or taller and men 6 feet (1.8 m) or taller. Models must be even taller than this for catwalk work.

MODEL SPEAK

Walk the walk and talk the talk with this fashionable guide to modeling!

BMI (body mass index)
a way of estimating the percentage of a person's body that is body fat

book
slang for a portfolio, or samples of a model's work

casting
an appointment to meet a magazine or company to see a model's suitability for a specific job

catwalk modeling
work during a high-end fashion show

catwalk show
an event where a fashion designer shows new clothes. Models walk on a catwalk so the audience can see the clothes from all angles.

collection
the clothes that a designer has made for a specific event or period of time, for example a spring and summer collection or an autumn and winter collection

commercial modeling
work targeted at selling consumer clothes or products, rather than high-end fashion

commission
the amount of money paid to an agent for finding work for a model

editorial modeling
work from a magazine's photo shoots that end up in its fashion pages

fashion week
a series of fashion shows that take place in a particular fashion capital, such as London (England), Paris (France), New York (New York), and Milan (Italy), to showcase new collections

go-sees
the visits models make to a potential client or photographer to get work

high fashion
the high-quality clothes made by top fashion designers

photo shoot
when a photographer takes pictures of a model for publication in a magazine or for use in an advertisement

Catwalk models jet around the world to appear at fashion shows during fashion weeks.

plus-size model
a model who wears a U.S. dress size of 10 or larger

portfolio
a collection of photographs that a model takes to go-sees. It shows a range of looks and the style of work a model can do.

runway
another word for a catwalk. It resembles an airport runway, because it is long and straight.

samples
clothes produced by fashion companies that are given to magazines before the outfits go on sale. This helps publicize new designs. Samples are tailored to fit fashion models.

tear sheets
a model's published work that has appeared in magazines

Vogue editor Anna Wintour is often seen in the front rows at major catwalk shows.

GLOSSARY

adrenaline
a hormone found in the human body that causes the heart to beat faster

annual earnings
the total amount of money that someone earns in one year

anorexia nervosa
an eating disorder where a person becomes obsessed with losing weight by not eating

body image
the perception people have of themselves when they look in a mirror

bulimia
an eating disorder in which people often overeat and then make themselves throw up

debut
a first appearance

discrimination
unfair treatment of someone because of his or her race, age, sex, or size

negotiating
agreeing about something through discussion

stats
short for statistics. In modeling, these are a model's measurements (height, chest, waist, and hips).

WORKING THE LOOK

From striking a pose in a magazine and looking larger than life on a billboard to strutting their stuff down the catwalk, models work in a variety of different jobs.

On the page

Editorial work consists of photographs that appear in magazines. It is some of the lowest-paid modeling work. However, the tear sheets, or pictures, that these shoots create are essential for a model's portfolio.

Perfect fit

In catalogs, models wear outfits from a store's collection. For high-end stores, showing clothes worn by models rather than just hanging outfits on racks or hangers is a huge boost to sales.

Ruling the runway

Catwalk modeling is the most demanding modeling work. Fashion designers require a specific look, and a catwalk model's career is short. Typically models work between the ages of 16 and 25.

Going global

Advertising is the best-paid work a model can do, especially TV commercials (known as TVCs). The model is paid a day rate for the work and is then given a series of further payments to allow the company to use the images or advertisement in different countries. One day's work can end up being worth hundreds of thousands of dollars if an advertisement runs for a few years around the world. It is like winning the modeling lottery!

To help catalog clothes look their best, designers choose the very best models who fit the sample sizes.

Editorial work requires models to adapt to several different looks and work with many photographers.

Celebrities such as actress Eva Longoria attract highly paid advertising work.

Catwalk models are taller than most editorial and commercial models—around 5 feet 10 inches (1.8 m) for women and 6 feet 1 inch (1.9 m) for men.

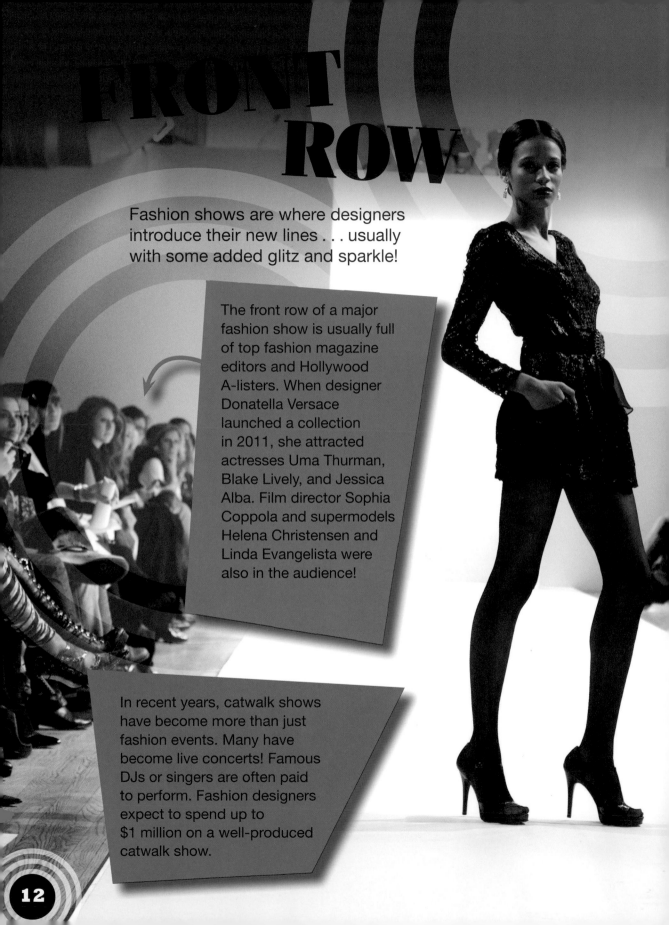

FRONT ROW

Fashion shows are where designers introduce their new lines . . . usually with some added glitz and sparkle!

The front row of a major fashion show is usually full of top fashion magazine editors and Hollywood A-listers. When designer Donatella Versace launched a collection in 2011, she attracted actresses Uma Thurman, Blake Lively, and Jessica Alba. Film director Sophia Coppola and supermodels Helena Christensen and Linda Evangelista were also in the audience!

In recent years, catwalk shows have become more than just fashion events. Many have become live concerts! Famous DJs or singers are often paid to perform. Fashion designers expect to spend up to $1 million on a well-produced catwalk show.

Designers very carefully select which outfits will be shown on the catwalk and in what order. They expect fashion editors to examine the look and style of their clothes and to appreciate the cut and the quality of each garment.

The fashion calendar revolves around major fashion shows in London, Milan, Paris, and New York *(shown here)*. Each city hosts two fashion weeks every year. More recently, important events have sprung up in Seoul, Korea; Toyko, Japan; Los Angeles, California; Hong Kong, China; Buenos Aires, Argentina; and Singapore.

Models are carefully selected for each fashion show. If a new model is lucky enough to catch the eye of a major designer, it can launch his or her career. Fashion models are chosen for how well sample size clothes fit them but also for their presence on the catwalk. Many top models have to master "the walk" before they can become a success on the runway.

Paris Fashion Week is held in the Carrousel du Louvre, an underground shopping center in the city. London's current location for most of its fashion week's events is Somerset House. New York's fashion week is held at the Lincoln Center for the Performing Arts.

ACTION FIGURES

Models work in a record-breaking business. Get the biggest, strangest, and most extreme stats in this larger-than-life world!

Sky-high model

Who: Amazon Eve
When: 2011
Where: Beverly Hills, California
What: World's tallest professional model
How: This personal trainer turned model entered the record books in February 2011 with her height of 6 feet 8 inches (2 m).

Keep walking!

Who: Copenhagen Fashion Week
When: 2010
Where: Copenhagen, Denmark
What: World's longest catwalk
How: Organizers of Copenhagen's Fashion Week entered the record books by turning a popular shopping street into their show's catwalk. Unlike a typical catwalk, which is 23 feet (7 m) long, the street is 1 mile (1.6 kilometers) long!

Jet-setter!

Who: Anja Rubik
When: 2010–2011
Where: Everywhere!
What: World's most in-demand model
How: This Polish catwalk model was ranked the busiest model in the world—appearing on 59 magazine covers and on 43 catwalks worldwide in a 12-month period.

Going underground

Who: Berlin Fashion Week
When: 2006–present
Where: Berlin, Germany
What: World's only underground train catwalk
How: Every year during Berlin Fashion Week, models for 20 different designers strut their stuff on the Berlin Underground for invited audiences as trains do circuits of the city.

Crowded catwalk

Who: Express fashion show
When: 2011
Where: New York City
What: Most models on a catwalk
How: U.S. clothing brand Express entered the Guinness World Records when 1,243 models walked down a runway in Times Square, New York.

Great brand loyalty

Who: Christie Brinkley
When: 1976–present
Where: Los Angeles
What: Longest modeling contract with one company
How: This U.S. supermodel became the face of CoverGirl cosmetics in 1976 and stayed with the company for almost 30 years, until she resigned in 2005.

Modeling veteran

Who: Carmen Dell'Orefice
When: 2011
Where: New York City
What: Oldest working model
How: This U.S. model celebrated her eightieth birthday—and 66 years in the modeling industry! She first appeared on the cover of Vogue when she was 15.

HOLLYWOOD MODELS

Everywhere you look, there's a magazine or a billboard advertising a fashion brand or fragrance with the face of a well-known celebrity. How did the trend start, and does it really work?

Instant recall

To keep sales healthy, companies need people to recognize and remember their product. Millions of dollars are spent creating this brand awareness to encourage shoppers to choose one product over another. Celebrities have helped increase product sales for years.

Scientists claim that seeing a celebrity in an advertisement can alter our thoughts, making us more likely to remember and buy that product. Actress Marilyn Monroe is credited as the first celebrity model. She was once asked what she wore to bed and replied, "Chanel No. 5, of course." The celebrity model was born!

Celebrities take over

Most mainstream model agencies have a special bookings section for the celebrities they represent. For example, Premier Model Management has a host of well-known faces on their books, from celeb Nicky Hilton to actress Lucy Liu.

Actress Drew Barrymore *(opposite)* is the face of cosmetic giant CoverGirl. Actress Emma Watson *(above)* models for Lancôme and Burberry.

It has also become common to see celebrities promoting several brands at once.

Working on the team

As more brands use famous faces, companies have to dream up new ways of making an impact. A recent trend has seen celebrities working for the companies they represent. Camera company Polaroid made pop star Lady Gaga a creative director last year, and Black Eyed Peas front man will.i.am is director of creative innovation for computer chip maker Intel. This way, companies get to use a celebrity's image and also tap into the creativity that made the celebrity famous.

SCARLETT JOHANSSON

The face the camera loves

THE STATS

Name: Scarlett Johansson

Date of birth: November 22, 1984

Place of birth: New York City

Lives: Los Angeles

Job: Actress, model

A Calvin Klein spokesman described Scarlett's advertising appeal as "hip, fresh, with an urban sophistication."

Child actress

The daughter of a Danish-born architect father and a film producer mother, Scarlett began acting when she was very young. She made her film debut at just nine years old and had memorable roles in the comedy *Home Alone 3* at the age of 13 and *The Horse Whisperer* with movie icon Robert Redford at the age of 14. Her breakthrough role came in 2003 with *Lost in Translation*, for which she was nominated for a Golden Globe Award.

Face of the moment

Johansson's on-screen success has led to offscreen opportunities. Her first big modeling break came in 2004, when the then 19-year-old actress was offered a two-year contract by Calvin Klein as the face of a new fragrance. In 2006 she signed a deal worth $4 million to be the face of cosmetics brand L'Oréal for a series of TV advertisements.

High-end fashion

More modeling followed, with famous luxury brand Louis Vuitton booking Johansson for two ad campaigns in 2007 for their spring/summer and autumn/winter ranges. She also appeared in Reebok's worldwide advertising campaign the same year. The sportswear giant also tapped into Johansson's creative talents by hiring the actress to help create a range of athletic-inspired footwear and clothing.

Perfect role

Johansson's role as an actress and model shows no signs of slowing down. Movie producers have recently cast her in crowd-pleasing action roles too. In 2010 she starred with Robert Downey Jr. in *Iron Man 2,* and she starred in *The Avengers* in 2012. The fashion world needs no convincing that she has the look and style to help sell their products. In 2011 Johansson appeared in her third ad campaign for Dolce & Gabbana's makeup line and her fourth campaign for fashion brand Mango (she has been working with both brands since 2009). Model-actress, or actress-model, Johansson plays both roles perfectly.

Career highlights

1994 made her film debut at nine years old in the comedy *North*

2003 received a Golden Globe nomination for her role in *Lost in Translation*

2006 appeared in TV ads for L'Oréal cosmetics

2009 named as the face of fashion brand Mango and Dolce & Gabbana's makeup collection

2012 starred in the comic book blockbuster *The Avengers* as Natasha Romanoff

MOST SUCCESSFUL MODELS

These women are the reigning stars of the fashion industry—from billboards to magazine covers, they've done it all.

1. Gisele Bündchen

Currently the most successful model in the world, with an estimated income of $45 million in 2010. Gisele grew up in the small Brazilian town of Três de Maio. At the age of 14, she visited São Paulo on a school trip. While there, she was spotted by Elite Model Management. Since then, she has worked with Dolce & Gabbana, Dior, and Versace and has appeared on more than 600 magazine covers. By the age of 30, Giselle had successfully launched her own range of sandals and beauty products.

2. Heidi Klum

With estimated earnings of $20 million in 2010, Heidi is a major fashion success. She won a national modeling competition in Germany before moving to New York to model full-time. She was the face of lingerie brand Victoria's Secret for 13 years. And since 2004, she has hosted the reality show *Project Runway*. Heidi has also launched a range of sportswear exclusively through Amazon.com.

3. Kate Moss

As Britain's best-known supermodel, Kate earned an estimated $13 million in 2010. At 14 years old, she was spotted by Storm Model Management. By the age of 18, she was appearing in advertisements for Calvin Klein and flying back and forth from London to New York up to eight times per week! In 2007 Kate began a partnership with retailer Topshop in which she designed her own range of clothes. This deal reportedly earned her $1.6 million per year.

4. Tyra Banks

After being spotted by a French model agent, Tyra skyrocketed to fame as an international supermodel. In 1996 she was the first African American woman to appear on the covers of *GQ* magazine, the swimsuit issue of *Sports Illustrated*, and the Victoria's Secret catalog. In 2003 she developed the reality TV show *America's Next Top Model*. Two years later, she started the Emmy-winning daytime talk show *The Tyra Banks Show*. After retiring from modeling in 2005, Tyra gained weight, something that critics were quick to attack her for. A longtime proponent of positive body image, Tyra embraced her fuller figure and launched the "So What" campaign to encourage healthier body image. Her estimated net worth is $90 million.

5. Naomi Campbell

At the age of 15, Naomi Campbell *(left)* began modeling. At just 18 years old, she became the first black woman to ever be featured on the cover of both French and British *Vogue*. She is said to be worth $48 million but is most famous as the woman who paved the way for other models of color to enter the world of fashion and catwalk modeling.

TYSON BECKFORD

THE STATS

Name: Tyson Craig Beckford
Date of birth: December 19, 1970
Place of birth: New York
Job: Model, actor, TV presenter

School days

Beckford was born in New York to a Jamaican father and a Chinese Jamaican mother. His mother was a part-time fashion model who often took him along to castings or to sit backstage when she had catwalk shows. In high school, Beckford enjoyed sports, but after leaving school, he had a series of jobs and hoped to one day become an actor.

Spotted in the park

In the summer of 1991, a writer for the hip-hop magazine the *Source* spotted Beckford playing football in a New York park. He was asked to model for the publication. From there, Beckford got an agent and started shooting his first fashion assignments for the the *New York Times*, *GQ*, and the department store chain Marks and Spencer.

Making it big

No one could have predicted what came next. In 1993 fashion icon Ralph Lauren chose Beckford as the face of his Polo line of male sportswear. Beckford was the first black male model featured in the company's advertising. The campaign was a huge success, and Beckford soon signed an exclusive two-year deal with the brand. In 1995 Beckford was named Man of the Year by music channel VH1 and one of the 50 Most Beautiful People in the World by *People* magazine. Campaigns with Gucci and Calvin Klein followed, and Beckford became the world's first male supermodel.

Face for film

In recent years, Beckford has spread his wings into TV hosting, acting, and producing. He has hosted the reality show *Make Me a Supermodel* and made appearances in several movies, including the modeling comedy *Zoolander* (2001), with actor Ben Stiller. Beckford has also helped to produce films including, *Kings of the Evening* (2008) and *Hotel California* (2008). Beckford may have retired from modeling, but his film work both on-screen and off-screen shows that he still loves the camera—and it still loves him!

BRAG

40th Annual Scholarship & Awards Gala

23

STAR HANDS

My story by Gemma Howorth

When I was growing up, people would comment on how attractive my hands were. It was weird really, and I didn't take much notice. Then my friend's mother, a professional photographer, said to me, "Seriously Gemma, your hands are better than all the girls I work with. You could be a professional hand model." So I decided to give it a try!

I started hand modeling in 2003. I set up my own model agency in 2008. The agency specialized in modeling particular parts of the body, such as lips, hands, and feet. Sometimes, I worked five or six days a week—a TV advertisement chopping carrots for a supermarket chain one day and appearing on the fashion pages of *Vogue* the next.

Every time you've seen a supermodel in a photograph with a hand on her face, 99.9 percent of the time, that hand will have been a hand model's. I've worked with Kate Moss quite a few times, with Lily Cole for Rimmel, and with Hollywood actress Rose Byrne for Max Factor. I had to lie on top of Rose for four hours with my little finger in her mouth! You wouldn't believe the jobs that I've done!

I've gone to extraordinary lengths to protect my hands. If I get a paper cut, I may be unable to work for two weeks. Whenever I cook, I wear a pair of dishwashing gloves, sometimes two, to avoid burns, and I always moisturize my hands 20 or 30 times a day. Almond oil is the best treatment to use because it moisturizes the cuticles too.

The work for body part models seems to keep increasing. Hand models are by far the busiest. With all the new smartphones and tablet computers, hands are needed to show the size of a product and demonstrate how it works. After hands, I'd say it was legs, feet, lips, and eyes in that order.
It really does make you think about modeling in a whole new light!

Gemma Howorth
—x—

JOY FATOYINBO

Joy grew up in Hamburg, Germany. He has worked for well-known brands such as Ikea, Debenhams, and Mini Cooper, among others. Here, he talks about life as a commercial model.

When did you start modeling?

I started at 23, which is very late! I was working in a bar in Berlin, and the owner, who was a photographer, took some pictures of me to advertise the bar. A friend put me in touch with a model agency, and they took me on.

What were you doing before?

I was training to be a lawyer. Even after graduating from college, there are several more years training. So I used my earnings from modeling to help fund my studies. I also managed to find work in cities such as Paris, France, and Cape Town, South Africa, which had busy modeling scenes. So I could combine my two passions!

Is there a secret to being successful at castings?

I wish! Your portfolio is very important—it's the center of your career so it needs to be kept up to date and have a good variety of images. A casting is like a job interview, so try to leave a good impression and make them remember you.

How do you feel when you don't get booked?

You can't take it personally. A lot of models find it hard to deal with rejection. But you have to realize that your face doesn't fit every job you try for.

What will you do when you retire from modeling?

I'll go back to law and set up my own legal practice. I'd say to anyone thinking of modeling, always have a fallback. An education is very important.

How do you look after yourself?

I go to the gym three times a week. It's hard because I'm a naturally lazy guy, so I have to drag myself there! I try to eat well and avoid desserts. And I try to get plenty of sleep, particularly the night before jobs and important castings.

VITAL STATISTICS

$250

The standard day rate for a *Vogue* shoot.

$45 MILLION

The estimated annual earnings of Brazilian supermodel Gisele Bündchen.

170

The number of countries showing the hit TV series *America's Next Top Model*.

1852

The year the world's first fashion model, French woman Marie Vernet Worth, appeared on a catwalk.

36–32–43.5

The stats of Kate Dillon, the first plus-size model to be shown in *Vogue*.

20 PERCENT

The standard commission that model agencies take from their models.

SIZE 0 ON THE CATWALK: YES OR NO?

YES

The fashion industry has been criticized for using female models who look underweight to advertise clothes. They are known as size-0 models. Designers say:

1. The models they use might look thin, but most are healthy and have a body mass index of 18 or more, which is considered normal.

2. Designers prefer to see tall, thin models wearing their clothes on the catwalk because they believe the clothes look better on slim models. Designers also believe customers prefer to see clothes shown this way.

3. It is hard to impose minimum measurements on models' sizes without being accused of discrimination. What about thin people? Shouldn't they be represented too?

4. Ultrathin models make up only around 10 percent of the fashion industry and are used mainly for catwalk shows. The fashion industry should not be criticized for this small number of models just because they are in the public eye more often than other types of models.

5. The industry is already doing a lot to promote diversity on the catwalk. In 2009 New York Fashion Week hosted its first show of plus-size clothes and London Fashion Week presented older and plus-size models.

NO

Critics say that size-0 models should
be replaced. They make these arguments:

1. Girls and women will be encouraged to aim for weight loss and
a body shape that is unachievable and unhealthy.
2. Successful plus-size models such as Robyn Lawley are better role
models for young women. The average U.S. dress size is 14, and
models who are a similar weight should represent them.
3. Maintaining a size-0 shape can be extremely dangerous. Several
fashion models have died because of health complications related
to drastic dieting and eating disorders such as anorexia nervosa
and bulimia.
4. Fashion magazines are forced to keep using size-0 models
because they are the only models who can fit into the clothes sent
by designers to be used for photo shoots. Designers should make
clothes for average-sized models and women.
5. The catwalk should reflect the diversity shown in the street—tall and
short, big and small, and young and old. There should not be just one
narrow view of what makes someone attractive.

YES OR NO?

Designers argue that taller and thinner
models make their clothes look better and
therefore help to sell collections. Historically,
tall, slender models have been used to model
clothes for that reason. However, when young
women compare themselves to models who
are seriously underweight, they may develop a
negative body image. As a result, they might
try to drop to an unhealthy weight. Models
should always be healthy, and no one's life
should be put at risk to follow fashion.

GET MORE INFO

Books

Banks, Tyra. *Modelland*. New York: Delacorte Press, 2011. Based on her own modeling experiences, Banks wrote this YA novel about the fictional, mysterious Modelland.

Beker, Jeanne. *Strutting It!: The Grit Behind the Glamour*. Toronto: Tundra Books, 2011. Get a behind-the-scenes glimpse of the modeling world.

Goss, Judy. *Break into Modeling for Under $20*. New York: St. Martin's Griffin, 2008. Read this book to learn how to break into modeling without breaking the bank.

Hill, Anne E. *Tyra Banks: From Supermodel to Role Model*. Minneapolis: Lerner Publications Company, 2009. Learn about Banks's rise to model superstardom in this book.

Thomas, Isabel. *Being a Photographer*. Minneapolis: Lerner Publications Company, 2013. Explore the exciting world of professional photography.

Websites

Elite Model Management
http://www.elitemodel.com/
Elite is one of the leading modeling agencies. Check out this website to see the agency's current models and to learn how you can be discovered!

Gisele Bündchen
http://www.giselebundchen.com/gisele_home.asp
Gisele Bündchen has propelled herself from being a supermodel to a business mogul. Visit her official website to see modeling photos and to stay up to date on her most recent business ventures.

Models
http://models.com/
Visit this website to see the campaigns and rankings of the current top models and to read up on current industry news.

INDEX

advertising work, 10–11, 17, 18–19, 21, 23, 24, 26, 29, 30
body part models, 24–25
bookers, 7, 17, 27
castings, 6–7, 22, 27
catalog work, 10, 23

catwalk shows 4–5, 10–11, 12–13, 14–15, 21, 22, 29, 30–31
celebrity models, 11, 16–17, 18–19
editorial work, 10–11, 28
fashion week, 13, 14, 30
go-sees, 6

model agencies, 7, 17, 20–21, 24, 27, 29
plus-size models, 29, 30–31
portfolios, 10, 27
scouts, 7, 20–21, 23
size-0 models, 30–31